30 DAYS OF GRATITUDE: A DAILY GUIDE FOR ADULT CHILDREN OF ALCOHOLICS

RON VITALE

CONTENTS

Let Go and Be Free Podcast   vii
Introduction   ix

Day 1   1
Day 2   4
Day 3   7
Day 4   9
Day 5   12
Day 6   15
Day 7   18
Day 8   21
Day 9   24
Day 10   27
Day 11   30
Day 12   33
Day 13   35
Day 14   38
Day 15   41
Day 16   44
Day 17   47
Day 18   49
Day 19   52
Day 20   55
Day 21   58
Day 22   61
Day 23   63
Day 24   66
Day 25   69
Day 26   72
Day 27   74
Day 28   77
Day 29   79

Day 30   81
Day 31   83

Sign Up for the Newsletter   87
Leave a Review   89
Also by Ron Vitale   91
About the Author   93

Copyright © 2023 Ron Vitale
All rights reserved.
Version: July 3, 2023
ISBN: 978-1-7368780-9-5
Visit Ron Vitale's website at www.LetGoandBeFree.com

LET GO AND BE FREE PODCAST

Come join others from around the world by listening to the free weekly podcast where you'll learn practical tips that will help you overcome your dysfunctional childhood upbringing and live a healthier life.

ronvitale.com/podcasts

INTRODUCTION

I grew up in a dysfunctional family. There was substance abuse, violence, and fear. For many years, I thought that the only way to overcome my past trauma was to find someone else to complete and love me. And worse, I used to find myself attracted to people who I tried to save.

I unknowingly recreated the abandonment and problems of my childhood upbringing with the same result: I'd be lost, afraid, and not understand why other people lived "normal" lives, but mine was anything but.

Yet once I started attending Adult Children of Alcoholics & Dysfunctional Family (ACOA) meetings, I realized that I wasn't alone. I studied ACOA's Twelve Steps and started going to meetings and therapy. I read self-help books, took interpersonal communication classes in college, and did my best to figure out what would "fix" me.

Little did I know that I didn't need to be fixed. I needed to be honest with myself, share and process (in a healthy way) my childhood upbringing, and then learn new ways to change unhealthy behaviors. It took time, lots of time.

I decided to write this book to share what I've learned over the past 25 plus years. The good news is that you're not alone. If you also grew up in a family where someone struggled with addiction and there were lots of dysfunctional behaviors, you've picked up the right book.

For many years, I felt a lot of shame about my childhood upbringing and tried everything I could to erase it from my past. I expect many people who know me don't know about my past because I became really good at hiding.

Only after I've had enough of feeling broken and lost, and embarrassingly weak in struggling with fear of abandonment, did I decide that I needed to find another way.

Instead of trying to erase my past, or cut it out, I chose a different path: integration and healing.

When I embraced my past and all of who I was, I realized that true healing could begin.

And the same is true for you: you are worthy of happiness, joy, and love.

You're not destined to suffer and continue to live in fear of your past. And there are skills you can learn to set strong boundaries if you still struggle with a family member who struggles with addiction.

This book contains a month's worth of self-reflections about gratitude that I found helpful in overcoming my childhood upbringing. You can read them in order or pick and choose randomly. It's up to you. The purpose of the daily reflections is to help you learn new ways of thinking and then take a few minutes each day to be grateful. Why? Some scientific studies have shown that giving thanks helps people feel better about their lives.

I invite you to come with me on this journey. Let's learn together and open our hearts and minds to a chance to heal.

DAY 1

Grateful for today.

Where to start? Some will start at the beginning, others will be on the journey already, and some will think they are finished, but need to start again. It doesn't matter where we are on the journey. All that matters is that we are here today.

Let's be grateful for today.

And there is no better place to start than to be thankful for this opportunity. You have carved time out to be here and to read through this book. When you look back on your life and allow yourself to feel the weight of the past, the truth is that you cannot change what has happened to you.

No amount of worry or thinking will change what has already happened. And the more you put energy into unhealthy relationships to try to "fix" the past, the more you will spiral out of control.

We cannot use the people and relationships in our life to time travel and fix our abandonment issues.

Instead, we can be grateful that we can acknowledge our past and our problems. Acknowledgement does not equal acceptance. What others have done to us may have been criminal, abusive, and destructive.

For today, we acknowledge all of who we are and embrace it. The way forward is through love and understanding this truth: as adults, we are now responsible for our lives.

We have the power and agency to choose to get help, to no longer be alone, and to love ourselves.

As we start on this journey together, let us take a moment to be grateful for where we are today. We may not be at the finish line, but that does not matter. All that matters is today. Not worrying about yesterday, 30 years ago, tomorrow, or six months from now.

Let us be thankful for this moment in time. Where we use our agency to embrace and hold up ourselves. Where we stand up and make certain that we listen to what we need, give ourselves the life that was withheld from us, and the stability of knowing that we will never abandon ourselves. We are here now.

To embrace the moment and be thankful for it allows us to see that there are boundaries that we can set. These simple questions can help us move forward:

- Is it true?
- Is this healthy for us?

At the beginning of our journey, our judgment might be clouded and it might be difficult to answer those questions.

You are not alone on this journey. Millions of people around the world carry their pasts with them, just like you, and let's be grateful for the opportunity to heal and be free of our pasts.

To acknowledge how we were hurt and to know that we can be whole and healed is enough for today.

. . .

I am grateful for...

1. ____

2. ____

3. ____

DAY 2

Grateful for knowing we are worthy of happiness and love.

For today's reflection, let's focus on being thankful for understanding that we need to accept all of who we are and to love ourselves in order to overcome the hurt and trauma we lived through as a child.

There is a silent, yet powerful, act that each of us can do every day.

When we stop chasing after others to have them love us, not abandon us, and we keep clean our boundaries instead of blurring our emotional needs with those of others, a calm will descend on us.

We do not need the acceptance of others to feel worthy.

We do not need others to know that we are loved.

When you sit alone with your thoughts, take a moment to breathe in through your nose, hold the air in your lungs, and think these words: "I am worthy. I am loved. I am me. There is no one else on the entire planet who is like me. I am unique, with all my flaws and quirks. I know from the deepest part of my inner self that I am grateful for this moment."

Then slowly exhale, and allow your fears, worries, and anxiety to leave your body.

We are human and messy. There will be good days and not so good ones, but through it all, we are still worthy and loved.

Why?

Because it is our quintessential truth: We are.

Out in the world there are many mechanisms to trick you into thinking: "You're not pretty enough, you're not thin enough, you don't have enough money, you're stupid, you need to buy certain things to be happy."

But none of that is true.

Our inner voice might have taken on the critical characteristics of the outer world's negativity.

We aren't stupid. We might have done something that was stupid.

We are brilliant, like the light of the sun on the first morning.

Too much?

Or not enough?

When we embrace the gratitude about who we are and love ourselves for the entirety of our messiness, that's when growth begins.

No one needs to come save us.

We have that power within ourselves. And if we don't know how to do that, then we can reach out for help. We can go to therapy or attend an Adult Children of Alcoholics & Dysfunctional Family meeting.

The beauty of realizing our own strength and embracing it is that it's okay to get tired, to need rest, to make a mistake.

Each day is a new opportunity to embrace the possibility of loving ourselves and to be free of the past. No matter how much we think or dwell on the past, we cannot change it. We will waste time, energy, and agency by getting caught in that mind trap.

The challenge is to learn how to truly believe that we are worthy of happiness and love.

The dark secret is that the little child in us might still believe that we were the reason why bad things happened to us as a kid.

But that's not true.

The sooner we break free of those damaging thoughts, the better.

Let's be grateful for the small step we're taking today: to love ourselves and embrace the possibility that we are worthy of a happy and good life.

I am grateful for...

1. ____

2. ____

3. ____

DAY 3

Grateful for forgiveness.

Let us sit still in the moment. Today, let's focus on being grateful for forgiveness. To forgive and be forgiven is a powerful act. Some choose not to forgive what their parents did to them. I have heard stories of abuse that made it clear that I have no right to tell another when and if they should forgive their parents.

I believe forgiveness is a private decision and one that needs to be freely given to another.

Rather than focus on who we can forgive and who has forgiven us, what if we stopped and were grateful for forgiving ourselves?

I forgive myself. I release the guilt, the shame, and the incessant fretting and worry that I spent in the past, trying so desperately to fill the sick abandonment needs that felt like a hole in my heart.

And you: What can you forgive yourself for?

What have you thought or said about yourself that you are ashamed of?

Do you feel trapped in a marriage? Are you enmeshed with a parent who struggles with addiction?

We all have said or done things that we regret. If we didn't, we wouldn't be human. We are imperfect, and that's okay.

The beauty of life is that we have the power to grant ourselves the healing salve of forgiveness. We can clean the slate, start fresh, and continue on our journey.

Forgiving ourselves is an act of mercy and love.

The challenge is to find the strength to continue onward and learn healthy behaviors for unhealthy situations.

Imagine a house. There are four walls, a roof, doors, all the items within, but there's also a foundation.

Being grateful for the act of forgiving yourself is the foundation for building your mental house. Without a solid foundation of love, trust, compassion, and forgiveness, how are we able to live a happy and healthy life?

When we look in the mirror, smile, and say, "I forgive you," there's a power there that's bubbling up from beneath the surface.

Having grown up in a dysfunctional family, I saw (and then emulated) many unhealthy behaviors. I learned codependency, enmeshment, reactionism, and how to worry and be afraid.

But I didn't learn how to solve arguments successfully and build up my own self-confidence.

I can forgive my past self as well as the "me" of the present.

We are strong, we are beautiful, and we are loved.

I am grateful for...

1. ____
2. ____
3. ____

DAY 4

Grateful for the Twelve Steps.

Today, let's be grateful for the Twelve Steps of Adult Children of Alcoholics & Dysfunctional Families World Service Organization. If you are not familiar with the steps, please take some time to review them at:

adultchildren.org/literature/steps/

No matter if you believe in God or not, there are important skills that the steps help you to learn. These skills allow you to learn behaviors that we didn't learn as part of our childhood upbringing.

I am grateful for not only the steps, but the people I have met at the various ACOA meetings I've attended over the years.

It is okay to doubt, question, and be wary of the Twelve Steps.

The steps are not a magic cure that will solve all your problems, but I have found that they are a guide that has taught me behavioral and communication skills.

When I look at the Twelve Steps and boil them down to their most essential nature, I've learned:

- To let go of the need to control things/people that I have no control.
- How to review my actions on a regular basis.
- Own up to admitting to my mistakes and making amends to people.
- Share what I've learned with others.

Instead of being lost and suffering, we can use the skills we learn through the Twelve Steps to carve out a new path for ourselves. Different doors are opened and we can learn that we are not a lost cause.

I searched for years to find a solution to my problems, but with the Twelve Steps, I found a toolkit that I could apply to everyday events and situations. No longer was I lost, alone, or felt broken. The power in the Twelve Steps is the realization that we are not alone. Others not only feel similar to the way we do, but they have used the Twelve Steps to live happier lives.

I'm grateful that decades ago, the first therapist I saw suggested that I look into the Adult Children of Alcoholics & Dysfunctional Family meetings. He shared with me information that helped me learn a new way of living. A way to break the generational cycle of dysfunctional from alcoholism and trauma.

I'm grateful and embrace the possibility of what today can bring when I allow myself the possibility of being free from my past.

What would happen if you read these words and embraced a similar possibility?

· · ·

I am grateful for...

1. ______________________________________

2. ______________________________________

3. ______________________________________

DAY 5

Grateful for knowing that we can't save others.

Let us be grateful for knowing that we cannot rescue or save someone else. We cannot stop our parents from drinking too much, can't solve our spouse's issues, and we can't save our children from any of their issues.

As much as we might want to swoop in and save the day, that's not going to help the situation. It might make us feel good (and needed), but going down that path lies codependency and unhealthy coping mechanisms.

When we spend our energy fixing other people's problems, we then lack the time and energy to help ourselves.

In a twisted turn of events, as adults, we can have the tendency to want to rescue and save others. Logically, it makes sense: no one helped us when we were kids and needed to suffer through the dysfunction we grew up with in our homes. Our parents may have been physically and emotionally unavailable to shield us from the effects of addiction and dysfunctional behaviors. Now that we're older, we have power and can use that to help others.

But jumping in to "save the day" isn't helping someone. Instead, taking on someone else's problems perpetuates unhealthy behaviors and creates enmeshment and codependency.

When we let go of other people's problems and focus on ourselves, change happens. We learn how to feel our feelings and not other people's feelings. We can reflect on what we want and need to be happy and to thrive.

Yes, it feels good to be needed and that rush of adrenaline can be addictive when we rescue someone. But how will we learn to set boundaries and take care of ourselves if we're saving others?

When we are grateful for recognizing that we struggle with codependency and enmeshment, the truth allows us the space to think and then act. Much of what we grew up with causes us to feel shame. We saw and experienced things that we never want to again.

So now we have a choice: We can work to learn about what happened to us growing up in an alcoholic and/or dysfunctional family, and use what we learn to heal ourselves. Or we can repeat the behaviors of our parents and continue the generational cycle of abuse and dysfunction.

Today, we can be grateful for the knowledge and awareness of where we came from and for seeing the path forward. The beauty of the journey toward healing and happiness is that we only have to take a step at a time. Sometimes it's only a second or two at a time.

Awareness and acceptance are the building blocks of a strong foundation for changing unhealthy and dysfunctional behaviors.

When we're closed off and in denial, we can't heal and grow.

So let's be honest with ourselves and admit that we can't save others. They are responsible for their own actions. And similarly, we can only save ourselves.

And with the setting of this boundary, we're on our way to a happier life.

One step at a time.

I am grateful for...

1. ____
2. ____
3. ____

DAY 6

Grateful for the realization that only we can heal ourselves.

What if we stopped and told ourselves: Today I am grateful for knowing that only I can heal myself?

Losing ourselves by looking to solve other people's problems isn't going to heal us. Using food and drink to numb our pain isn't either. And no matter how much we try to use outside sources (TV, adrenaline, anger, denial, etc.), none of this is going to solve our problems.

I believe that only by telling our story, and processing what we've lived through, can we learn how to overcome the problems from our childhood.

When you live in an alcoholic or dysfunctional family, sometimes it was hard to know what was true, whom we could trust, and what was "normal." As kids, we may have used any type of coping mechanism to survive. But over time, we became older and started learning what did and didn't work anymore.

I remember being in my early 20s and thinking: "Hmm, I'm

seeing a pattern in my romantic relationships. There's a period of infatuation that's so intense and feels so free and alive, but then everything crashes and falls apart. Why is that happening?"

That's the self-realization that I'm grateful for.

When we stop and look at our lives, we then realize that we need to do the work to heal ourselves.

For me, no romantic relationship was going to fix the problems I had in feeling abandoned by my father. I needed to find out why I felt that way, how to overcome it, and then learn new skills to put into practice.

All of this took time.

But it's not impossible.

I went to therapy, started attending Adult Children of Alcoholics & Dysfunctional Family (ACOA) meetings, and learning how to self-parent. I needed to learn how to love myself and I did that by trial and error. I needed to make room for myself. What exactly does that mean?

Instead of filling the hurt inside by throwing my whole self into a romantic relationship, I needed to figure out what to do with my feelings. I went to movies by myself, talked with trusted friends, went to ACOA meetings, listened to music, wrote in a journal, and took care of myself.

I made time to eat, exercise, and sleep.

Before, I would stay up late, not get enough sleep, and used the rush of a relationship as a salve to try to heal myself. But none of that worked.

How could it?

We are responsible for our own healing. We have to choose to take care of ourselves.

But let me be clear: If you're dealing with depression, healing might mean talking to a therapist **and** working with a psychiatrist to take an antidepressant. I'm not a medical professional. I can't say what will or won't work for you.

I do believe that one of the first steps toward overcoming your childhood past traumas is coming to the realization that your happiness and health are in your hands.

There is power in realizing that and I hope that, for today, you take a moment to think about that thought.

I am grateful for...

1. _______________________________________

2. _______________________________________

3. _______________________________________

DAY 7

Grateful for one thing about ourselves.

What is one quality that you have that you like and are grateful for?

Taken out of context, you might wonder why this is important, but I would suggest that setting the stage for a healthy balance depends with an honest look at ourselves.

What do you like about yourself and why?

Being grateful for who you are is the foundation of building up strong self-confidence and helps us see that we do not need another to feel completed.

If we felt abandoned or neglected in growing up, one of the ways to overcome our feelings of hurt and fear is to focus on taking care of ourselves.

Here, in the present, we are in control of our choices and where we go from here.

And we have many choices.

We could become narcissistic and put up our defenses so that we go through life making sure that we get everything we want without a care for others.

Or we might put the needs of others over our own and lose ourselves along the way.

When we take time to be grateful for even one quality, the focus is turned back on us and lets us reflect on who we really are.

Are you grateful for a physical quality or psychological?

Are you strong? A good listener? Empathetic?

When we hit a bump on the road of life and encounter a problem, the voices from our past might creep back up on us and might be difficult to block out. Did your parents call you stupid or rage at you after they drank heavily? Were you blamed for problems?

In my years of talking with other people who identify as Adult Children of Alcoholics, I've heard many such stories. The guilt and the shame associated with those memories is a heavy burden to bear.

What I ask of you today is to counter program those old memories and create new ones.

By practicing on a regular basis, you can listen to your own voice instead of falling back on the hurtful memories of your past.

When you make a mistake, you're not stupid, but the mistake was stupid.

Remember that.

Building up your self-confidence and learning to self-parent to overcome an unhealthy childhood upbringing takes time, but can begin with one small step.

What did you like about yourself and are grateful for?

Might seem silly in the beginning, but building up your self-confidence will help you not just today, but in the years ahead.

I am grateful for...

1. ____

2. ____

3. ____

DAY 8

Gratitude for love.

I'm going to focus on being grateful for love in my life. I ask you to join me with this today. But I might not be coming at this from where you think.

Yes, it's wonderful to be in love and have that special someone in your life.

Maybe you don't have that, maybe you do.

For today, I'm asking you to put love from others to the side and for you to focus on yourself.

Love of self.

Some people in my life have cringed when this topic comes up, but I ask you to come with me today.

Before we go any further on today's reflection, let's take a moment and say the loving-kindness meditation:

May I be happy
May I be healthy

May I be peaceful
May I live with ease

Silently read (or speak out loud, if you feel comfortable doing so) the meditation. By growing up in a family environment where people struggled with addiction or there was lots of dysfunction, we didn't see healthy ways that family members loved themselves.

We have scars and struggled with trauma, abandonment, hatred, fear, and a whole list of feelings.

But someone teaching us that it's okay to love ourselves, and how to do that? Well, that probably didn't happen much (or at all).

When we admit that we have so many questions and don't know where to start, and don't know what being "normal" is or really even means, that's the perfect opportunity to try.

If your thoughts are filled with negative self-talk and you've been put down your whole life, finding the courage to embrace love can be scary.

I get it. I really do.

It is not our fault that those who raised us struggle with addiction. We cannot solve their problems. We cannot save them, and we're also not to blame.

What we are responsible for is figuring out what we want to do with our lives, and that starts right this minute.

Now.

No one can wave a magic wand and take the weight off your shoulders and make you feel better.

The good news: All you need to do today is to start going on the journey. If all you can do today is read the loving-kindness meditation three times, that's a great start.

When a child learns how to walk, it takes time. When I was teaching my children how to walk, we started with "tummy time" when they were little. From there, my kids learned how to roll over, then they started crawling, and eventually they started walking (wobbling at first, falling on their butt, and then getting back up again).

When the negative self-talk rises up within you, feel it, then let it go. Say the loving-kindness meditation, practice what it means to love yourself.

"I love myself."

Say it.

That doesn't mean that we feel it or believe it. Unlearning the dysfunction that we grew up with will take time.

If you need help, it is okay to ask for it. Make an appointment with a therapist, attend an Adult Children of Alcoholics meeting, or talk with a trusted friend. All of these are a few examples of how to get help.

Learning how to love yourself is a skill that you can use for the rest of your life.

How to get there?

Make space in your heart for the possibility that you are worthy of love.

That's where we'll start.

I am grateful for...

1. ____

2. ____

3. ____

DAY 9

Gratitude for boundaries.

A boundary can be like the walls of a prison cell, or as open as the Earth's atmosphere (but integral to our survival since we all need air to breathe).

When we take time today to be grateful for boundaries, let's reflect on what they do for us and how to practice using them.

Here are several common situations that come up in life:

- Your boss comes to you and asks you to work later, but you already have plans to see your kid in the school play.
- Your longtime friend meets up with you and talks your ear off. She is having problems with her husband and she is over sharing with you.
- Your spouse wants to spend a major holiday with his family, but you want to spend it with yours.

Each of these examples can be stressful, and depending on the strength of your emotional boundaries, could cause lots of trouble.

I grew up in a dysfunctional family and it was a lot easier being a people pleaser. Don't rock the boat, do what was asked of you, and then I could go on my merry way. The problem, though, is that I learned (the hard way) that at work and in other relationships, that people will take advantage of people pleasers.

When I didn't stand up for myself, then no one else ever had my best interest at heart. At work, if you don't learn to say "no," then you will continually be put upon and overworked.

Finding the right balance between shutting everyone out in your life and having no boundaries at all takes practice and time.

I find the Serenity Prayer (attributed to American theologian Reinhold Niebuhr in 1943) to be extremely helpful:

"God, grant me the serenity to accept the things I cannot change, the courage to change the things I can, and the wisdom to know the difference."

If a situation comes up that's stressful for me, I run the prayer through my head: What can't I change? What can I? And how do I know the difference between the two?

And for those who don't believe in God, simply omit the first word of the prayer. There's still plenty of goodness in the sentence to help you think about where your boundary ends and where someone else's begins.

Why is that important?

Because that's how we learn the difference between codependency and being enmeshed with someone else's feelings, and our own thoughts and feelings.

There are times when we might need to take a stand for ourselves and take care of ourselves. That's okay.

The beauty of boundaries is that we can link self-parenting and self-love with practicing our boundaries.

When thrown in a problem or situation, we can use the Serenity Prayer and line that up with this question: Is this healthy for me? Along with: Is it true?

These touchstone questions can help guide us as we learn how and when to strengthen our boundaries. In the beginning, we might have weak boundaries, then we might have them be too stringent. But over time, we'll learn how to modulate our boundaries as we navigate through life.

Sometimes we'll need stronger boundaries with certain people, and weaker ones with others. Why?

We will have some people in our lives who respect our boundaries and will not test or push past them, whereas some people might try manipulation, lie, or use emotional tricks to get through or around our boundaries.

Yes, it's complicated, but for today, let's be thankful that we have the power to control who and what we want to do in life. And if you're not quite there yet, then you've taken another step forward by learning about boundaries and on how to practice using them.

I am grateful for...

1. ____

2. ____

3. ____

DAY 10

Gratitude for time.

Today, please join me and let's be grateful for time. Time to learn how to live happily and be free from our past.

Time to forgive ourselves.

To learn how to love, to let go, to unhitch ourselves from the cycle of generational trauma.

Each day that we are alive, we have an opportunity to start again, to learn, grow, love, and be.

When I look back at my childhood, I see how closed off I was. I didn't understand why life unfolded like it did. I only knew that I was caught up in a dance of destruction.

My father's untreated traumas bled into his relationships and that affected my whole family. I felt so trapped, lost, scared, and confused.

What is your story?

Time takes place now.

Right now.

Casting our mind back to yesterday, last year, or decades ago is a trap that loops us in a false sense of security, but it's really a prison of the mind.

"If only..."

Those words can be used in thinking about the past or the future.

"If only she didn't drink too much..."

"If only she could stop drinking and get help..."

Time.

We have time now. We cannot go back and undo history. We can't rewrite their wrongs. We can't project ourselves in the future and stop them from drinking. And the more time we spend worrying about the past or the future, the more we'll waste our chance for the here and now.

We have time today.

Time to learn to let go of the past, to heal from it, and to break the multi-generation cycle of dysfunction that addiction has caused.

But how?

I hear you.

When we are willing to let go of who we were, and to embark on a new path, that's when we begin to change.

Here's an example to help you. I used to spend hours thinking about my past and felt broken about how my father had abandoned us. I used to cry when I would think about how I never had a "normal" upbringing. My father wasn't there to teach me how to throw a ball, ride a bike, teach me about dating, or how to be a kind and loving man.

So I searched and searched, in all the wrong places, for a way forward, but I always circled back to the past and felt trapped there.

But when I chose to go to therapy and talk about my pain and then started going to Adult Children of Alcoholics & Dysfunctional Family meetings, I learned that I wasn't alone and then could practice skills on how to overcome my pain.

The skills I learned saved me.

I learned how to communicate effectively, how to heal from my feelings of abandonment, and to love myself and actively self-parent.

Learning all this took years.

And that's why I'm grateful for time today.

Each second is precious because it's a step forward toward a happier life.

I am grateful for...

1. ____

2. ____

3. ____

DAY 11

Gratitude for letting go.

Let's be grateful for letting go and admitting that we can't save those we love who struggle with addiction or some other dysfunctional behavior.

I remember when I first learned about the Twelve Steps and I struggled with giving up control in my life. Because I had such a rocky childhood, I wanted to know exactly what was happening and when.

It made no sense to me to let go and to admit that I was unable to help someone else.

What I didn't understand then is the difference between myself and others.

Even writing that today seems nonsensical.

Of course, I understand that I was a different person than someone else, but when I started dating, I became attracted to people who struggled with their own issues and thought that I could save them. And that through some sort of warped thinking, that by my saving/rescuing someone in the present, that it would somehow heal me of all the past trauma that I had lived through as a child.

Does that make sense?

No, it doesn't, but it is what it is.

I'm not ashamed now to admit that I struggled with this need to rescue those I "loved." When I peeled away what was going on, I had to come to terms that I was trying to control someone else and use them to fix my own problems.

But for today, take a look at your life and the relationships you have with your family members. Are you able to let go and admit that you can't rescue them?

The more energy and time we spend trying to solve someone else's problems, the less we have for ourselves.

When we let go and focus on our own physical, spiritual, and mental health, we set up the conditions for us to be free from our past.

The more we try to fix, rescue, or save others, the more we'll continue to perpetuate our sufferings.

What can we do differently?

Let go and stop trying to control or save others.

Instead, use that time to heal ourselves through learning healthy behaviors.

Want a specific example?

I'll give you three:

1. Write in a daily journal.
2. Meditate or pray.
3. Take care of your body and mind (eat, sleep, and laugh).

These might seem simple or the most difficult thing in the world. The trick is that there is no trick: healing from our past takes time and replacing unhealthy coping mechanisms (trying to save people) with healthy ones.

. . .

I am grateful for...

1. ______________________________________
2. ______________________________________
3. ______________________________________

DAY 12

Gratitude to accept help.

Gratitude comes in all forms. When I was young, I felt alone, lost, and scared. But as I grew older, I learned that others struggled from also growing up in a family that dealt with addiction and dysfunctional behaviors. For the longest time, I thought that I had to do everything on my own.

But that's not true.

Sure, I needed to take the steps to get help and to do the work, but there have been people to help me along the way.

I have worked with therapists as well as people in support groups who were kind enough to listen to my story (without judging me). And I remember my first sponsor when I started attending Adult Children of Alcoholic and Dysfunctional Family meetings.

He was kind, patient, and willing to teach me.

What I remembered the most from him is that he volunteered to be my sponsor by helping me learn the Twelve Steps and to be a guide for when I needed help in those early months. We would talk, and at the end of our meeting, he'd offer me a hug. We'd hug, and he said to me, "Most men hug like this." (He then pounded my back and quickly backed away like most men do—seemingly afraid of giving a true hug.) But then my sponsor gave me a real hug. He held me close and ran his hand in a circle on the top portion of my back.

In that moment, two men held each other, and I realized that this is what it would have been like to have my father hug me.

And through my sponsor's teachings, along with those of my therapist at the time, I learned that I could build a healthy network of people in my life who could help support and teach me.

My journey began when I went to therapy for the first time after a bad breakup. My therapist and I saw each other for a few sessions and then he suggested that I attend an Adult Children of Alcoholics meeting. Eventually, I gathered up the courage to do that and met my sponsor. From there, I went on to try different meetings and met a bunch of other people who have helped me on my path.

I didn't need to do it alone.

So, for today, let's be grateful for knowing that others can teach and help us—if we're open to it.

I am grateful for...

1. ____

2. ____

3. ____

DAY 13

Gratitude to get help beyond us.

There's a moment in time that is enshrined in my memory: I felt my heart had broken. I had been dumped. I felt lost, upset, and confused.

But I realized that I needed to go and get help.

I could no longer pretend that I had all the answers and that the way I was living life was working for me.

So I chose to go to therapy.

And through therapy, my therapist taught me about the Adult Children of Alcoholics meetings.

I am so thankful that there are ways to find healing and help.

Some will turn to God, some to therapy, some to the books of self-help experts—where do you turn to?

I am grateful that I am able to step back and have an honest look at my life.

I know that I'm far from perfect, have my faults and quirks, and I now know what skills I need to practice, where I can learn new things, and how the world is filled with such beauty and life.

It all started with a simple thought: I need help.

When I was younger, I used to think that I could do everything on my own. I had the intelligence, strength, and the brashness of youth to think that I could "will" my problems away.

But what I didn't factor in is the power of the warped, unhealthy behaviors that my dysfunctional upbringing had taught me.

I didn't understand what being normal was and found it confusing on how to solve relationship problems.

Instead of acting when problems came up, I'd react.

Need some examples?

If I was at work and a problem came up, I'd want to try to solve the problem and jump in to solve it. I had such weak boundaries that I'd think nothing of working extra and putting my heart and soul on the line.

Or when I was in a romantic relationship, when my partner would be dealing with her own problems, I'd want to fix it. I'd offer advice and assistance, thinking that it was my responsibility to help solve her problems.

I didn't understand that the best way to be present in a relationship was to work on my own issues and give space to my partner. To listen, be empathetic, but not to react. Sometimes the best way to be was to be supportive, validate that you hear what they're going through, and get out of their way.

Each of us is on a journey. We can choose to stay trapped in the dysfunctional cycles we learned as kids, or we can try a new path.

The subtle difference between yesterday's reflection and today's: awareness and action.

Yesterday's reflection focuses on realizing that others can help us and today's reflection is acting on getting that help.

Take a leap forward, or the baby step, it's up to you.

I am grateful for...

1. _______________________________________
2. _______________________________________
3. _______________________________________

DAY 14

Gratitude for self-reflection.

What is right and what is wrong? Depending on your upbringing, you might have received mixed messages from your parents. Maybe you saw infidelity, experienced domestic violence, sexual abuse, or a whole litany of painful moments.

So where does that leave you today?

Let's close our eyes and be thankful for an ability to self-reflect. What happened to us in the past and what we do in the present are separate and different.

If we make a mistake today, hurt someone's feelings, or take out our pain against ourselves, we are responsible for our actions.

When we take the time to self-reflect, we need to have a guide to compare ourselves to.

The beauty of being free in this moment is that we have the power and agency to self-reflect and ask ourselves: Did I hurt someone else? Have I hurt myself?

There is no one to judge us in the silence of our own mind.

When I spend too much time helping others and not making enough time for me, I'm setting up an unhealthy pattern for myself. If I lose my temper with my kids, I am responsible for that.

Before we can make amends, we first need to have made an inventory of the things that we have done.

Did you cheat, did you steal, did you curse at someone, or did you call yourself stupid?

The purpose of self-reflecting is to come clean with any unhealthy behaviors that we've committed and are honest with ourselves.

Sometimes that's easy to do, while other times it's more complicated.

Being grateful for a chance to self-reflect takes courage and the willingness to shed the light of truth on your actions.

It's not helpful to berate yourself for being "bad." That's not what we're doing here. Doing something bad or immoral is one thing, but we aren't "bad."

Taking a step to coming to terms with our limitations, our mistakes, and times where we actively made decisions to hurt someone else's feelings is the stepping stone to building a foundation of honesty and respect.

If we do not first respect ourselves and aren't honest with how we're acting, how are we to grow and learn healthy ways of dealing with the problems and challenges we encounter in life?

Being grateful for time to self-reflect allows us the opportunity to grow and mature. We are perfectly imperfect, and that's the beauty of our existence. We have self-awareness, but often are blind to our own faults because we used unhealthy coping mechanisms to survive our dysfunctional upbringings.

Today, let's be grateful for the opportunity to be truly honest with ourselves and embrace all of who we are.

. . .

I am grateful for...

1. ____
2. ____
3. ____

DAY 15

Gratitude to admit when we are wrong.

I went to Catholic school all through elementary and high school. I read the bible more times than I can remember. One of the passages that I liked was Matthew 7:5:

"First, remove the beam out of your own eye, and then you can see clearly to remove the speck out of your brother's eye."

It is easy to bolster support when we can point to what others did to us. We can have true and incontrovertible facts that we were wronged.

Yet seeing our own faults might be harder.

Are we controlling? Manipulative? Deniers?

When we take time to stop, self-reflect, and then admit to ourselves and the world our wrongs, we have a chance to overcome them and become healthier.

Even if you don't struggle with some form of addiction, there is a possibility that you have taken up the characteristics of someone who does. Why?

Because we become what we know—unless we choose to break the cycle.

And to do that, we need to reflect on who we truly are and admit where we are wrong.

Why would we ever want to be grateful to admit when we've done something wrong?

Because then we know what we need to work on and can create a plan to overcome those aspects of our personality.

For years, I tried so hard to cast out the "bad" parts of my personality. I tried to shed my anger at my father, and what I came to realize is that when I tried to cut that anger out of me, I wasn't accepting why I was so angry. And when I'd run into a problem in life, I found myself wanting to control whatever the situation was or using anger as a defense.

But when I began to embrace my full self (even those parts of my personality that I was ashamed of), my world changed.

The same can be true for you.

The first step is to admit the quintessential nature of our wrongs.

From there, we can learn how to heal from our past and integrate new (and healthier) ways of dealing with our problems.

It might seem odd, but embracing an opportunity to admit our flaws is the path toward healing and resolution. The more we try to deny or run from our problems, the more they'll catch up with us when we're in a time of crisis. We fall back on what we know and repeat behaviors until we shed light on what's not working for us, and then learn a new way.

Pointing out another's faults, but ignoring our own, is the surest way to stay trapped in a cycle of dysfunction.

.   .   .

I am grateful for...

1. ____
2. ____
3. ____

DAY 16

Gratitude to be willing to change.

Today, let's be grateful for being ready to grow and change.

What does this mean?

For years, we may have put up our defenses and looked out and pointed a finger at everything done to us. And that may have served us well for a long time. But we are older now, and at some point, we need to come to terms with our own issues and problems.

This does not mean that we belittle or lessen the trauma that happened to us while growing up in a dysfunctional family.

But we can't simply point at those past memories and use them to blame for why we act the way we do now in the present.

Our past may have shaped and influenced us, but that does not mean that we need to stay limited and trapped. Or worse, we don't wish to repeat the generational cycle of dysfunction.

To overcome repeating the patterns of the past, we first need to admit that we're ready to grow beyond the defects of character that hold us back.

What's a "defect of character?"

Here are a few to get you thinking: Using denial to not address a problem, fear of being on your own due to abandonment issues, expressing anger to stunt yourself emotionally, lying to yourself that "everything is fine," stuffing your emotions down and replacing openness with emotional eating, or trying to save others instead of working on your own issues.

These are just a few to get you started. The point here isn't that we go through a long laundry list of what's "wrong" with us, but to be open to honest and effecting change.

We can choose to stay on the path we are on and feel superior because we have a slight bit of self-knowledge, but if we don't admit that we're ready to grow beyond our defects of character then we'll be doomed to repeat them time after time.

When we encounter a situation that is stressful, we'll fall back on our tried-and-true behaviors and the pattern of dysfunction will repeat itself again and again.

But when we are ready to have our defects of character removed, that can be life changing.

How?

Because when you are willing to admit that you are not perfect and are willing to learn new ways of handling problems, opportunities arise.

Imagine a couple caught in each other's gravity: one person drinks too much and the other person nags the other. Round and round they go with the same result: nothing changes.

But what happens if the person who drinks too much starts going to AA and commits to living the Twelve Steps and becomes sober? Or what happens when the other person stops trying to change the person who drinks too much but works on their own issues and decides that they need to be responsible only for their own actions?

The unhealthy bond between the two of them is weakened and will eventually break.

Granted, life often isn't as simplistic as my example, but I wanted to focus on a simple point: change is possible for everyone.

Before we can change, we need to be willing to change. And in order to be willing to change, we need to be honest with ourselves about what our defects of character are.

Once we do that, anything is possible.

I am grateful for...

1. ____

2. ____

3. ____

DAY 17

Gratitude to have our shortcomings removed.

At the height of the pandemic, I used to go on long runs and wonder what the future would be like. I'd get to a road near my house and struggle as I had to run uphill. Since the hill was about halfway through my run, I had to slowly build up the strength in my legs to not only complete the hill, but also to finish an even larger hill at the end of the run.

To do that, I'd slowly run onward and think about the future. On a good day, I'd imagine sending energy, love, and happiness to my future self. Since I didn't know what would happen with the pandemic, I just did my best to imagine a time when we were no longer in quarantine and that the worst of the virus was over.

On bad days, when my legs were tired, I'd imagine reaching out to me in the future and taking energy from myself to help me in the present.

My little game helped me because I was able to focus on something outside of the present situation. I imagined that there would be a day that was better than the present and to get to that point, I knew that I had to put one foot in front of the other (literally).

The same is true with overcoming any of our shortcomings: we need to do the work to get us to a better place.

Today I am grateful for the power of help. That help could come in the form of prayer, hope in yourself, or through professional experts—or a combination of these.

The point is that we have an opportunity to embrace a new way of life. A new way of being. We are not stuck in the same ruts and trapped to repeat what our parents struggled with when we were kids. Sometimes we might feel that we are destined to repeat the mistakes of the past, but that's only an illusion.

Part of what's necessary to overcome our past is a belief that we can be happy and that we are worthy of happiness.

When we're grateful for the removal of our shortcomings, this belief sets off a chain reaction within us. We can grow beyond what we know. We can live with love, joy, and be at peace.

But first, we need to believe that our dream is even possible.

Do you believe that?

If not, why not?

I am grateful for...

1. ____

2. ____

3. ____

DAY 18

Gratitude to be willing to make amends.

Today, let's be grateful for the willingness to be able to make amends to anyone in our life who we had harmed.

Why would we be grateful for this?

Because in order to grow, we need to take accountability for the mistakes we've made.

Most of us probably know someone who refuses to admit that they're ever wrong. The thing is: we all make mistakes.

As I like to say: "We are perfectly imperfect."

We will never be perfect, but we have a chance to see that we can work with others on the road of life and do our best to live life in happiness and goodness with love.

What I used to want so much as a kid, I could never have. I wanted my father to apologize for all that he had done to our family and for him to get the help he needed.

That never happened and for a long time I carried that secret wish along with me, hoping that my life would change for the better. And when I became older, I carried a lot of baggage from my past. I made lots of mistakes along the way in not knowing how to be in a relationship. I kept trying to fill that need to fix my past abandonment issues by falling in "love" and then trying to save my romantic partner.

And it was all for naught.

When I realized that I needed to first take care of myself and stop using relationships to complete me, things changed in my life. I became aware of my imperfections and that led me to a spot where I became open to making amends to others in my life.

Being open to apologizing and showing (through actions) that we're sorry for what we did to hurt others, and then put our new behaviors into practice is a big commitment and can be difficult.

But it's not impossible.

Imagine a day where you can come to that decision where you're ready to list out the people you have harmed and are willing to admit that you've made mistakes and will own up to it.

That can be a scary moment, but it's always one of great freedom and joy because we will be able to free ourselves from the past. We can then chart a new course and work to exhibit healthier behaviors as we go about our lives.

This does not mean that we are perfect and won't make mistakes again, but it does mean that we have committed ourselves to doing the work of self-parenting and learning the necessary skills to regulate our emotions, being honest and the courage to admit when we make a mistake.

Coming to a point of honesty within ourselves does not mean that we wave a magic wand and suddenly everything is fixed with a sprinkle of magic fairy dust.

But here's the good news: we have the opportunity to try again, to grow stronger, learn new communication skills, and to practice them. Sounds messy? You bet it is. But that's the beauty of life. We can celebrate the journey.

. . .

I am grateful for...

1. ____
2. ____
3. ____

DAY 19

Gratitude to make amends.

As we go through life, there's a point when we can be self-centered, other-centered, or a healthy balance between the two. To find the right balance between only thinking about ourselves or being overly involved in other people's lives, we need to practice building up our boundaries and looking at how we interact with the people we love in life.

When we are willing to change our unhealthy behaviors and actively work to be forgiven for the hurt we have done to others, that's the turning point that signals a shift in our universal understanding of accountability.

We go from blaming others for our problems to accepting that we are responsible for our own behavior.

Why be grateful for this?

It's simple: To admit when we have hurt someone's feelings and to work with them to resolve the conflict lays the groundwork for stability and peace.

A long time ago, a professor in college told me that they had always wanted an opportunity to talk with someone whose feelings they had hurt. But the person had passed on.

If you have an opportunity to ask someone to forgive you for something you've done to them, take up the chance. Not to simply say "I'm sorry," but to also let them know that you're willing to change. You don't plan on treating them the same way again. You can show them that you have grown, learn better listening skills, and are able to more effectively communicate in the relationship.

Real growth comes about through change.

If a husband constantly belittles his wife when they get into a heated argument, his asking to be forgiven is the first step. The second, and more important act, is to show his wife that when they next get into another disagreement that he stops belittling her. Instead, he can share why he's lashing out that way. Maybe the situation is triggering a memory from his past and puts him on the defensive? So instead of trying to undercut her by belittling her, he can listen, be honest in how he feels (using "I" statements such as "I feel scared about not having enough money because this reminds me of how little money we had when I was a kid and I was afraid my parents would lose our home.").

However, keep in mind that not everyone is ready (or wants) to forgive us.

When someone tells us that they don't want to speak to us or to offer their forgiveness, we need to respect that person's wishes.

Gratitude to making amends comes in understanding that we have the power to change and actively show someone else and ourselves that we do not have to be stuck in the obsessive and destructive patterns we learned from growing up in an alcoholic or dysfunctional family.

We can grow, become aware, and change.

Not because someone wants us to, but because we've learned a healthier and happier way to live.

· · ·

I am grateful for...

1. ____
2. ____
3. ____

DAY 20

Gratitude to have the power to self-reflect each day.

Let's be grateful for being able to look deep into ourselves and admit when we make a mistake.

When my kids were little, I made a point of going up to them when I made a mistake, apologizing to them, and telling them that I would do my best next time. I'm not perfect, and I never will be, but I have the ability to be a decent human being.

For me, that means being honest, treating people (that includes myself) with respect, and sharing love with others.

As kids, we were often dragged into a circle of addiction and dysfunction. We had no power to overcome what our parents were going through.

But that's not the case any longer.

We can choose to be trapped by the past, or to learn ways to integrate the past into our lives, and live healthier and happier.

When you start out on the journey, it's frustrating because you want to feel better right away. You might look around and see how happy people are in commercials, TV, and on social media and ask yourself: "Why can't I feel that way?"

Remember, there's an illusion all around us as people often are only showing their good side to the world. We often don't know the struggles that people are going through behind the scenes.

The responsibility that we have is to first take care of ourselves. To get to a better place, we need to learn new ways of self-regulation and on how to process past trauma.

Worrying about how long that might take only zaps the joy out of life.

Instead, for today, we have the power to self-reflect, see what we might have done wrong, and admit it to others. That might include when we've treated ourselves badly.

There are many paths to feeling better and overcoming our dysfunctional family upbringings. The question is: What path will we take?

Therapy? Attending Al-Anon or Adult Children of Alcoholics meetings? Meditation? Daily pages? Exercise? Eating healthy? Self-care activities? Getting enough sleep?

There are many paths and that's okay.

When we weave together a network of positive behaviors that will help us learn how to overcome the past, then we can practice them a little each day. It might be a slow process. Incrementally slow some days, and lightning fast on others.

That's the beauty of life—we don't quite know what tomorrow might bring.

But for today, let's take some time to self-reflect, go through our recent behaviors, see if we hurt our own or another's feelings, admit to it, and move on.

Slow, steady, and consistent.

It'll be okay.

. . .

I am grateful for...

1. _______________________________________
2. _______________________________________
3. _______________________________________

DAY 21

Gratitude for using prayer or meditation to connect with the universe.

I can't please everyone. It's just not possible. But I can be truthful and open with you. Maybe you believe in God. Maybe you don't. It's not for me to say what is right or wrong for you. Only you can figure that out.

For me, I've struggled with religion. I grew up in a Catholic family and went to Catholic schools through most of my education, but then decided to leave the Church at around the age of 19. My reasons are my own and I have shared them on my podcast (ronvitale.com/podcasts).

There are days when I believe more fervently in God than anything, and there are times when I don't.

I struggle with God because I don't understand why there is so much suffering in the world and why a God would allow that. I am dispirited by the manipulation and abuse acted out on innocents in the name of God.

So, to be fair, my belief in God is complicated.

For today, I ask you to be grateful that you have a choice to believe in God or not.

Whatever decision you make, focus on that belief and then use prayer or meditation to help you come in contact with God (or life within the universe) so that you can better understand what your purpose is and the strength to live toward that purpose.

Anyone can be a destroyer in life.

But to find purpose in building and in connection, that takes effort and strength.

What if you don't believe in yourself? What if you feel that you're not worthy? Not capable or destined for love? Not good or smart enough?

This is why I ask you to pray or to meditate.

Such negative constructs are barriers created by the unhealthy behaviors we learned as children growing up in an alcoholic and/or dysfunctional home. We learned what we saw and we've internalized unhealthy behavior and replicated it, often in the attempt to survive.

Now we are at a fork in the road. We can pray, meditate, think (whatever works for you) and find connection with God, the universe, or our innermost and quintessential self.

The truth is that each of us is whole and complete. We are worthy of love, unadulterated joy, and fulfillment.

When we realize our full potential and live it, that is when we break from the past and start living in the present, and take the first steps into a life of fulfillment.

For me, I will say this today:

Oh God, help me to understand who I am and what I am meant to do in this life. Help me to better accept myself and the strength to live up to my full potential. I pray that I will hear you, be open to you and the people in my life who will guide me toward my life's goal. I ask you to help me see clearly not only what I'm meant to do in life, but the strength to walk forward, and the awareness to know when I need to rest and be kind to myself. The love I so desperately wanted when I was a kid is already within me. When I am weak and tired, help me to know that I love myself. I love you. I love the world. Thank you.

This is my secret prayer. What is yours?

I am grateful for...

1. _______________________________________

2. _____________________________________

3. _____________________________________

DAY 22

Gratitude for the ability to share our journey with the world.

Let's be grateful for having received the opportunity to learn about the Twelve Steps of Adult Children of Alcoholics and being open to sharing what we've learned with others.

This does not mean that we force feed the message to those we meet, but we show through our behavior what we've learned.

Show don't tell.

As a kid, my mom would say to me: "Your father used to say 'I'm sorry' to me time and time again, but he'd still wind up doing the same bad things over and over. I was sick of hearing him apologize. I wanted him to change."

Now, as an adult, I take that lesson to heart. There is great power in not just memorizing the Twelve Steps, prayers, or tenets of enlightenment.

Real change comes when we put into action what we've learned.

We don't go around with a big sign saying: "Hey, look what I've learned."

Instead, put into practice the knowledge you've gained about regulating your emotions, harnessing the power to set healthy boundaries, communicating effectively, along with the tools you're gaining on how to resolve conflicts.

All of this comes slowly, over time.

Brick by brick, layer upon layer, build upon your successes and share what you've learned with your family, friends, and then your wider community.

I am grateful because I have learned how to be healthy in a relationship that's built on trust and love.

This is where the power of all our work comes to its fruition and that gratitude shines from within.

To go from being trapped in a life where we can't find our way out of dysfunction, hurt, fear, and anxiety to living a life of happiness, truthfulness, and love is priceless.

There are so many people who suffer right now. Children and adults who do not know that there is hope.

That is where we come in.

We become the light that shines the way.

As impossible as that might seem now to you, we have the power to grow beyond the trauma that has held us back and shaped our lives to live a full and healthy life.

That's why I ask you to be grateful for today: the possibility of sharing our journey to the world.

I am grateful for...

1. _______________________________________

2. _______________________________________

3. _______________________________________

DAY 23

Gratitude for not being a people pleaser anymore.

You are allowed to say: "No."

If one of your parents or a partner tries to guilt trip you, manipulate, or passive aggressively get you to do something for them, saying "no" is an acceptable answer.

And that does not mean that you owe anyone a long explanation as to why you can't help. Set the boundary, say "no," and that's it.

When you can be grateful for no longer being a people pleaser, doors will open for you. You are then able to spend time on yourself. Self-care is critical.

To always do the bidding of an alcoholic parent or a troubled sibling is not healthy for you. Don't allow people to manipulate you. Take a hard look at your life and ask yourself: "Is there a person that I am helping out too much?"

There is a difference between helping someone and enabling.

The world changes when you set that hard boundary line and

refuse to play the game of getting wrapped up in the drama of someone else pulling you into their one-person show.

Imagine the day when you realize that you're done being a people pleaser and that you don't need someone else's appreciation to feel good. Imagine how you'll feel when you come to terms with your own unhealthy need for validation from someone else.

Imagine saying the word: "No."

Not: "I'm sorry but I can't…"

You have no need to apologize, you have the right to deny a request. You have the right to take care of yourself. You have the right to be happy.

Is it easy to stop being a people pleaser?

No, it's not. It takes practice, a plan, and patience.

Today, let's focus on the power to stand up for ourselves and to focus on our own needs (and not the needs of others).

Sometimes loving someone else means that we need to stand up for ourselves first and let them face the consequences of their own actions. Shielding them from the unhealthy decisions they've made isn't going to save or help them.

What's it going to do?

It'll create an unhealthy relationship where you are enmeshed with someone, and that means that you're not spending the time and energy to take care of your own needs.

Not sure how to get to that day when you're no longer a people pleaser?

Start small.

Take the first step: say "no" to something that you really don't want to do.

How to figure out what's healthy or unhealthy for you?

Ask yourself this question:

Is it healthy for me?

And then be honest with your answer.

.   .   .

I am grateful for...

1. ____
2. ____
3. ____

DAY 24

Gratitude for letting go of anger.

A parent is supposed to love you, care for you, support you, and always be there for you. But, unfortunately, if you grew up in an alcoholic or dysfunctional family, that's not true. Emotional, physical, sexual, or verbal abuse may be more in line with your reality.

Over the years, I know that I harbored a lot of hatred and anger for what I had to live through. I'd see what other people's families were like and wish that mine was normal.

But that wasn't the case and it would never be true.

I held anger within me so that I felt like I could take a piece of coal and crush it into a diamond. I wanted nothing more than to have a fairy tale family life, but that was never going to happen.

As much as I wanted my family life to be normal, there wasn't anything to be done to fix that, and I carried a lot of resentment for many years.

Over time, I learned to accept my anger, listen to the hatred, and learn to let it go.

The paradox of hating someone who was my parent ate away at me for many years. I tried to cut that part of me out, but the more I tried, the more I failed.

How could I unbecome who I was?

And then I learned the secret: I embraced all of who I was. The hatred, the fear, the anxiety, the worry, as well as the love, hopefulness, and joy.

The day that I learned to let go of what my father did to our family was the day that I started to become free.

And I will be forever grateful that I gave myself the space to heal. No matter how much I tried to go back and fix the past by recreating similar relationships in the present, nothing could heal the pain that I had lived through.

Only by learning a new path of facing my fears and pain did I find a way to grow and heal.

Whatever your situation is, you have a choice. As broken you might think you are, and as dark as your childhood may have been, today you can find help and a way to heal.

How?

Acknowledge what happened to you, list out where you need to learn new behaviors (by unlearning unhealthy coping mechanisms), and get help.

Some options: Talk with a professional, attend an Adult Children of Alcoholics or Al-Anon meeting, or incorporate healthy habits into your daily routine. For me, that meant a combination of all these options over time.

Take a step forward today.

We will all fall and make mistakes, but it's embracing our imperfections and truly loving who we are (past and all) that sets us on a path of living a fulfilling and happy life.

The moment we stop looking for a parent or a proxy relationship to fulfill us, the sooner we realize that being comfortable with ourselves is the way forward.

And that starts with being grateful that we can let go of the anger and hatred at those who hurt us.

I am grateful for...

1. ______________________________________
2. ______________________________________
3. ______________________________________

DAY 25

Gratitude for Þetta Reddast - it's going to be okay.

I am grateful for learning something new. I came across the Icelandic saying Þetta Reddast (pronounced thet-ta re-dust) that roughly translates to "it's going to be okay." In the 2023 World Happiness report, Iceland ranks third in the list. That's pretty high up, so I think there's something worth investigating there. In comparison, the USA (where I live) ranks at number fifteen.

Being open to learning and applying new skills helps us chart a new course from what we learned growing up in families where addiction and dysfunctional behaviors affected us.

The World Happiness report breaks down people's happiness around the world and is a great resource for understanding why people are happy.

It's worth a read. The good news is that you can get the free report at worldhappiness.report.

But what about Iceland's famous saying Þetta reddast?

In a country that's shrouded in darkness much of the year, has bitter cold, and volcanoes, the Icelandic people learned not only how to survive against such a harsh environment, but they took their suffering and found a way to transform it into a positive attitude.

When you put in the work of self-care and healing from your past trauma and match that with a survivor's attitude (e.g., "it's going to be okay"), you set yourself up for a healthy and happy future.

In my experience, I wasted a lot of time worrying. I used worry as a way to prepare for the worst. But by worrying too much, I lost the ability to enjoy life. I became too focused on what might happen and how I could prepare for that.

Taking a cue from the Icelandic people, saying Þetta reddast ("it's going to be okay") gives us the space to focus on what we can and cannot control.

At some point, we need to let go and choose to focus on the positive.

But as a kid, I didn't believe that things were going to be okay because of my family upbringing. I truly didn't know how things would turn out.

Each of us has a choice: we can choose to do the work to overcome our past or we can perpetuate the cycle of dysfunction.

I hope that you choose the former.

Life is challenging and can be hard. There's no doubt about that.

And saying "it's going to be okay" isn't a magical mantra that's going to take away all our problems. But when we add saying Þetta reddast to our toolkit, we expand our options toward setting ourselves up for a happier life.

And that's why I'm grateful for learning something new: there's hope for each of us.

I am grateful for...

1. ____
2. ____
3. ____

DAY 26

Grateful for community.

I grew up in a dysfunctional family and for many years, I felt lost and alone. I closed myself off from the hurt and figured that I'd go forward in life as best I could. Back in my teens and early 20s, I didn't know that there was a community of people out there who felt similar to how I did.

After I attended my first few Adult Children of Alcoholics & Dysfunctional Family meetings, I met people from all walks of life. I met the young and the old, and people who looked different from me, but I realized that we had our upbringings in common.

The power of the ACOA community taught me that by coming together, we could help each other through listening and supporting.

The shared connection we have with learning the Twelve Steps is the central tenet that helps guide us in life.

No longer did I need to be alone and lost and confused.

And today, I can find lots of people in ACOA groups on Facebook.

When you're first starting out, it's easy to think that something's wrong with you. Or to think that you are broken and not worthy of love and happiness.

But none of that is further from the truth.

We are whole and worthy of love and happiness.

It might be difficult to see through the fog of the chaos that we grew up with, but there are tools at our disposal to learn healthier ways of living.

We do not have to react to the dysfunction in our lives. We can choose to act.

Being reactive puts us on the defensive and often leads us to choose dysfunctional responses to problems.

We do not need to be stuck in the past or limit ourselves.

The power of community can help us learn a new path, one without codependency, enmeshment, or self-sabotaging behavior.

Taking the first step is hard. I get it. I really do.

The choice is up to you.

I am grateful for...

1. ____

2. ____

3. ____

DAY 27

Gratitude for who we are.

We are who we are. We were born and lived through all sorts of challenges to get to where we are today. We are not perfect and that's okay.

Today, let's be grateful for ourselves.

The journey that we're on has been filled with ups and downs, but you're reading this passage, so know this: there is no one else like you on the entire planet. All that you are—the good, the mixed, and your personality quirks are uniquely yours.

What if you took the time each day to be grateful for who you are?

What if you realized that to be happy, you don't need someone else to "complete" you?

What if you embraced all of who you are and truly believed that you are whole and beautiful inside and out?

We are not damaged goods.

We are filled with limitless possibilities and the essence of love.

We cannot go back and fix what happened to us as children, but we can embrace ourselves today and love ourselves for who we are. The love that we didn't receive from our parent(s), we can have today.

If we wear sunglasses inside all the time, but were to take them off and see the true world around us, that can give you a glimpse of life's tremendous opportunity and reach.

We do not need to be defined by our past and we are not stained by what our parent(s) did (or still do). Addiction and dysfunction may have wrecked our childhoods and affected us as adults, but there is a way to live a healthier and happier life. The path forward has many avenues, but one that's pretty consistent is loving ourselves.

To be grateful and fall in love with ourselves is foundational. This is not a narcissistic type of love where we ignore the feelings of others around us, but a wholesome and balanced love that heals and is selfless.

As weird as it might sound, stand in front of a mirror, hug yourself, look yourself in the eye and say: "I love you. I accept you for all that you are and will be here for you, no matter what."

There is power in knowing that you will not abandon yourself.

The little child within you will smile at that.

In a way, parts of our personality were frozen in time because of the trauma we lived through. But when we spend time on self-care and self-parenting, we allow ourselves to heal.

But how?

While growing up in a family that suffered from addiction and dysfunction, our needs were neglected. As adults, it is not possible to go back in time and relive our childhood and to erase the past.

Instead, we can use visualization techniques and affirmations to heal our wounds.

Here's a simple exercise: Imagine that the adult you meets up with you as a child. Kneel down, say hello to your childhood self, hug them, and say, "I will never leave you. I love you and everything is going to be okay."

Use this visualization technique when you feel scared, worried, or upset.

We are able to heal and live lives filled with happiness and love.

Today, it starts with celebrating and embracing all of who we are.

I am grateful for...

1. ____
2. ____
3. ____

DAY 28

Gratitude for being alive.

Today, let's be grateful that we are alive. Let's put aside the problems in our lives and the things that we see wrong with the world. How often are we spending time worried, anxious, or upset about things beyond our control?

If you're reading this, then you're alive.

Every breath that we take in is a chance at renewal, growth, happiness, and love.

We don't know for certain how or why we were given the gift of life and consciousness. But we are the only beings that we're aware of who can think and put words to our thoughts.

The opportunities that we each have are limitless.

I wish that I could wave away all my problems, but I can't do that. And I can't take away any of your problems.

We could spend hours listing what struggles we have, but what would that bring us?

For this moment, let's be grateful that we are alive.

Close your eyes, take a slow and deep breath in through your nose for a count of four, hold that breath and mentally count to five, and then slowly exhale through your mouth for around six seconds.

Repeat this two more times and then open your eyes.

We are unique, worthy of happiness and love, and a miracle.

The challenge that we struggle with is that we grew up in a family that struggled with alcohol and exhibited dysfunctional behaviors.

Yet here we are today, survivors who have a chance to embrace life, and can not only choose a new path to live a healthier life, but we can spread that message of hope to others.

The joy of being alive allows us to see the beauty in a sunset, hear the giggle of a young toddler's laugh, smell the fresh baked bread as it comes out of the oven, and feel the cool rain as it comes down on us during a summer storm.

We are one of billions on a beautiful blue planet orbiting a yellow star in a distant quadrant of the Milky Way.

When we put aside our problems and take a moment to embrace the beauty of being alive, we can, if even for the briefest of moments, feel connected to all that is.

And that is good.

Today, take a moment, embrace those few seconds, and allow yourself the freedom to feel alive.

I am grateful for...

1. ____

2. ____

3. ____

DAY 29

Gratitude for realizing that saving people isn't love.

The bible says that love is patient, and that it is kind. I rather like that. Love is not saving someone who is damaged and that we rescue.

When I was a teenager and in my early 20s, I found myself attracted to people who I thought needed to be rescued. I'd fall in "love" with them, throw myself into the relationship, and then I'd try to rescue them.

What could go wrong?

Actually, a lot.

Not only did I lose respect for myself, display a lack of boundaries, but then I would get angry when the person didn't want me to "save" them.

None of it made sense to me at the time.

But once I started going to therapy and attending Adult Children of Alcoholic (ACOA) meetings, my life began to change. I learned how important it is for me to take care of myself and solve my own problems.

I am not, nor will I ever be, responsible for "fixing" someone else. People are not playthings to fix.

I have done my best to make amends to the women I tried to rescue while we dated. And I have forgiven myself for trying to recreate that pattern of abandonment that I lived through as a kid.

In some unhealthy cycle of dysfunction, the adult child in me wanted to go back to when I was abandoned, and fix it by reliving similar events in the present with the women I dated.

It took a long time, and some honest looking in the mirror, for me to realize that I needed to change.

I am so thankful and grateful that I had learned that trying to save someone hurts and disrespects the woman I tried to rescue, and I devalued myself.

I felt a lot of shame about how I acted and how broken I felt after those relationships dissolved. All I wanted was to love and to be loved. I tried so hard to "fix" things. But I lost everything in the end.

Once I hit rock bottom, I realized that I had discovered a healthy way to live and to find love.

First, I needed to heal myself. It took time, work, and patience, but it is possible.

Whatever you struggle with, whatever the burden, first you need to admit where you need to grow, forgive yourself, and then learn a new way to live. That last part can be tricky.

For me, therapy, attending ACOA meetings, and learning about the Twelve Steps helped me.

What can you try today?

I am grateful for...

1. ____

2. ____

3. ____

DAY 30

Gratitude for feeling stable and at peace.

Once I started taking care of myself by attending Adult Children of Alcoholics (ACOA) meetings and studying the Twelve Steps, I discovered that my life began to change. At first, I didn't really notice it, but then I started seeing a pattern. I stopped being attracted to people I wanted to rescue or save, I steered clear of drama in relationships (be they at work or among my friends), and I finally figured out what living a "normal" life meant.

I didn't go from crisis to crisis.

Today, I ask that you be thankful for seeing a new way to live. A life where you can find stability and be at peace.

For some, being at peace and living a stable life might seem impossible, but it's not. There is a way to do it.

It takes time, patience, and work.

I like to think that just as a farmer sows his seeds and raises his crops, I have put effort into my life so that I am now living a bountiful life.

When we stop arguing about the same old issues, let them go, and take care of ourselves, whole new opportunities become possible.

Though it takes practice, setting strong boundaries with people allows us to find the strength to stop being a people pleaser and gives us the emotional strength to avoid being sucked into an alcoholic parent's cycle of dysfunction.

The strength that we find within ourselves is a gift of unending love. We are not beholden to whether someone loves us or not. Our value is not derived by rescuing others or feeling needed.

The beauty of living a stable and peaceful life is that we learn how to handle the bumps we encounter on the road of life.

Problems will pop up and when they do, we will have the skills in our toolkit to solve them.

Even if we backslide and fall into old patterns, we then can take time to regroup, and right our wrongs. We're not trapped, helpless, or alone.

We have ourselves and the ACOA community.

There is strength in numbers.

No matter what stage of the journey you are on, please know that there is hope. You are not alone. You are worthy. And best of all, you are loved.

I am grateful for...

1. ____

2. ____

3. ____

DAY 31

Grateful for endings.

I wanted to include one additional day for the book. Why? Getting a little surprise is fun, but there's also a practical matter. Some months have 31 days and I thought it would be helpful to cover every single day for those months of the year.

I used to think that endings were extremely sad. Because I grew up in a dysfunctional family and struggled with abandonment issues for many years, I've had a difficult time in saying goodbye.

My grandmother used to say: "Don't say goodbye, say so long. That means you'll see that person again."

I don't know why she believed that, and she's since passed on, so I can no longer ask her.

But how I think about endings has changed over time. Before, I used to get really stressed out about endings, but now I see that sometimes I want things to end. And at other times, saying "so long" to someone doesn't mean that I won't ever cross paths with them again.

Right before my son was born, we lost my father-in-law and both my grandparents mere months before his birth.

I grieved each of my loved one's passing and realized that I also have all of their memories within me. And now, with cameras and mobile phones, I have lots of pictures and videos of loved ones who have died.

None of us know when we will leave this Earth and there's no way for us to know when someone who has an addiction will choose to get help and work on themselves.

What we do know, as I've started this book, is that we have today.

We might not have tomorrow or the day after. And there's no use getting all worried about the future. No matter how hard we try, we can't control what's going to happen. Sometimes accidents happen and bad news comes our way.

Endings are simply the start of another beginning.

I used to hate it when people told me: "when one door closes, another opens," but it's true.

We can choose to learn new communication skills, process our past trauma in therapy, and practice new behaviors so that we don't repeat the mistakes of our alcoholic and dysfunctional family upbringing. Is it easy? No.

I would rather work toward a lifelong goal and be happy than to take a shortcut that would only leave me at a deadend. But that's me.

If I hadn't started on my journey more than 25 years ago, I wouldn't have started writing the *Let Go and Be Free* books, started the podcast, or written this book.

Just because this book is ending doesn't mean that it's over and everything each of us needed to learn has been completed.

I'll be learning up until the moment I pass on.

Once we start the journey of healing and empowerment, we realize that we have a say in some of our endings.

We can decide to leave a toxic job and start another.

We can put up strong boundaries with a parent addicted to alcohol and choose self-care.

We can end allowing our fears and worries to control us.

Those endings can be cast off so that we can open a door to a new beginning.

I've written this book in such a way that you can get to the end and then start right over, or you can randomly pick a passage each day.

You are in control and can decide what you want to do and how you want to end this book.

It can end right now—just finish and put it away, or you can start again at your own pace.

With books about empowerment, self-reflection, and healing, I have found that reading the book again after a bit of time is extremely helpful because I'm not the same person.

Each day I'm slightly different from who I was the day before.

I like thinking about that because that means that there is hope.

There's hope for each of us that we will grow beyond the problems we grew up with and hope that we will have the scales pulled from our eyes and will truly see, experience, and believe how wonderful life is and how we are worthy of immense happiness and love.

We were born to love and we can start that this moment.

Let's put an end to always searching for someone to fix us and truly and deeply love ourselves.

I am grateful for...

1. ____

2. ____

3. ____

SIGN UP FOR THE NEWSLETTER

Sign up for the free weekly newsletter and get tips on dealing with unhealthy behaviors, links to resources and the *Let Go and Be Free* podcast.

ronvitale.substack.com/subscribe

LEAVE A REVIEW

Thank you for reading this book. I would appreciate your leaving an honest review. Your review will help other readers like you find books they love!

ronvitale.com/30days

ALSO BY RON VITALE

Let Go and Be Free: 100 Daily Reflections for Adult Children of Alcoholics (Volume 1)

Let Go and Be Free: 100 New Daily Reflections for Adult Children of Alcoholics (Volume 2)

Let Go and Be Free: 100 More Daily Reflections for Adult Children of Alcoholics (Volume 3)

Let Go and Be Free: 100 Final Daily Reflections for Adult Children of Alcoholics (Volume 4)

ABOUT THE AUTHOR

Ron Vitale is a fantasy and science fiction author. Influenced by the likes of Tolkien, Margaret Atwood, C. S. Lewis, and Philip Pullman, he has a Master's degree in English Literature from Villanova University where he studied the works of Alice Walker and Margaret Atwood. For his thesis, he interpreted Walker's and Atwood's novels through a psychological Jungian approach by showing how the central female protagonists use storytelling as a means to heal themselves from trauma. He lives in a small town outside of Philadelphia, Pennsylvania, and keeps himself busy by writing his blog and on learning how to be a good father to his kids, all while working on his next book.

Learn more about all of the books written by Ron Vitale at www.ronvitale.com

www.ingramcontent.com/pod-product-compliance
Lightning Source LLC
Chambersburg PA
CBHW061426050726
47593CB00006B/2251